This Journey Belongs to:

....

Date:

....

Present
-OVER PERFECT-

GUIDED JOURNAL

JOURNEY TO A SIMPLER,
MORE SOULFUL LIFE

SHAUNA NIEQUIST

ZONDERVAN®

ZONDERVAN

Present Over Perfect Guided Journal
Copyright © 2021 by Shauna Niequist

Requests for information should be addressed to:
Zondervan, *3900 Sparks Dr. SE, Grand Rapids, Michigan 49546*

ISBN 978-0-3104-5683-4 (hardcover)
ISBN 978-0-3104-5684-1 (audio)
ISBN 978-0-3104-5682-7 (ebook)
ISBN 978-0-3104-6062-6 (signature edition)

Author is represented by The Christopher Ferebee Agency, www.christopherferebee.com.

Zondervan titles may be purchased in bulk for educational, business, fundraising, or sales promotional use. For information, please email SpecialMarkets@Zondervan.com.

Art direction: Sabryna Lugge
Cover Design: Curt Diepenhorst
Cover photography: Aaron Niequist
Cover calligraphy: Lindsay Letters
Author photo: Sarah Carter
Interior Design: Denise Froehlich

Printed in the United States

21 22 23 24 25 LSC 10 9 8 7 6 5 4 3 2 1

A CHANCE TO REMAKE YOUR
LIFE FROM THE INSIDE OUT

*My prayer is that this guided journal
experience will be a thousand invitations
springing up from every page, calling
you to leave behind the heavy weight of
comparison, competition, and exhaustion,
and to recraft a life marked by meaning,
connection, and unconditional love.*

Contents

Introduction

I wrote *Present Over Perfect* as an account of my winding, messy journey from exhaustion to peace, from isolation to connection, from hustling and multitasking to sacred presence.

I hit a point in my mid-thirties when I realized that there were all these words I wanted my life to be: connected, warm, spontaneous, meaningful, graceful, rest-filled—but my actual life was rushed and frantic and isolated and exhausted. I was an extremely busy, productive person, but I wasn't the friend, the wife, or the parent I wanted to be, and I realized that the trade-off wasn't worth it. It just didn't matter to me anymore that people thought I was very responsible and very capable; I wanted to reclaim a life of connection and play and rest.

I've failed miserably and begun again, asked for help, asked for grace, asked for prayer. And beyond those things I've *done*, the more life-altering parts of the work are those things I've *not done*: the moments that I've allowed—or forced—myself to stop, to say *enough*, to rest, to breathe, to connect. That's where life is, I'm finding. That's where grace is. That's where delight is.

In this journal, I'm sharing bits and pieces of the *how* of my journey: the questions I asked myself, the habits I shook off and replaced with gentler rhythms, and the path I walked back to dwelling deeply in God's love. If *Present Over Perfect* was a hand reaching out across the pages, inviting you into that same journey, then this journal is the friend that walks the dusty road alongside you so that you don't have to go it alone. This is the beat of my heart: to experience grace and nourishment and to offer them, one in each hand, to every person I meet. Grace and nourishment. Rest and space. Connection and love.

I want you to know that it's better here, in this place of love. This journey has brought about a meaningful transformation in every single part of my life. My prayer life, my marriage, my family life, my friendships. I enjoy my work more. I feel a deep well of gratitude, a clean and grateful desire to live a life of meaning. I have the energy to dedicate myself to the things that matter to me and that God has called me to. I have the security to truly rest, to truly enjoy this extraordinary world and all its offerings—books and art and meals and people and conversations and cities and beaches and night skies.

In the space that used to be filled with a whirring ball of anxiety, now there is a new patience, a new settledness. The deep well of contentedness that I feel these days is nothing short of a miracle, and it's one I am thankful for every single day. My prayer is that this journal can be a meaningful guide along your own path toward growth and grounding.

What are you longing for?

> I was missing the very things I so badly longed for: connection, meaning, peace. But something kept driving me forward—a set of beliefs, routines, and instincts that kept me pushing, pushing, pushing even as I was longing to rest.

What beliefs, routines, or instincts are holding you back?

Sea-Change

The term sea-change *is from Shakespeare's*
The Tempest: *a man is thrown into the sea,
and under the water he is transformed from
what he was into something entirely new.*

've come to believe that there are a handful of sea-changes in our lives—experiences that transform us, passages from one season to another where the old is gone and the new is come. For me, this latest sea-change has been about moving from frantic and frayed living into peace, connection, and rest.

This journey is never *finished.* But you can be fundamentally changed, rebuilt from the inside out, leaving behind ways of living you may have once believed were necessary but were, in reality, truly toxic and damaging.

My life is marked now by quiet, connection, simplicity. A peace defines my days, a settledness. I searched for this in a million places, all outside myself, and was astounded to realize that the groundedness is within me and perhaps was there all along. Now I know that the best thing I can offer to this world is not my force or energy but a well-tended spirit, a wise and brave soul.

Now I know there's another way. And that other way is possible for you too.

How have you experienced sea-changes in your life?

What inciting incident plunged you into a new way of living?

....
....
....
....
....
....
....
....
....
....
....
....
....
....
....
....
....
....
....
....
....
....
....
....
....

> No one ever changes until
> the pain gets great enough.

I'm not at all an "in my head" person. I'm a smell and taste and feel and grasp-between-my-fingers person, and both life around the table and life on the water are ways of living that I experience through the tactile sensations of them, not the ideas that float above them.

How would you describe yourself? How do you best relate to the world?

What would be lost if you slowed down to a pace that felt less like a high-speed chase all day, every day?

What would happen if you trusted that there would be more time down the road for all of those things you feel *must* be done?

If someone gave you a completely blank calendar and a brimming bank account, what would you do?

Which words describe what you ache for these days?

What does fake-resting look like for you?

> So many of us don't know how to truly, deeply rest. We only know how to fake-rest. It may look like we're resting because we're wearing pajamas, but really we're ticking down an endless list, sometimes written, always mental, and constantly getting things done.

What would it look like to truly allow yourself to rest?

What feelings are you trying to outrun? What is the ache inside you that you haven't wanted to face?

Which activities do you rely on to outrun your feelings?

1. ....
....

2. ....
....

3. ....
....

4. ....
....

5. ....
....

6. ....
....

7. ....
....

8. ....
....

9. ....
....

10. ....
....

What are some of the stories you believe about yourself? Are those stories helping you or hurting you?

The story:

HELPING   HURTING

The story:

HELPING   HURTING

The story:

HELPING   HURTING

The story:

HELPING   HURTING

The story:

HELPING   HURTING

Which words would others use to describe you?

Which words do you *wish* they would use?

A pastor of a fast-growing church was telling the story of how the church had exploded, how they couldn't stop the growth, an inexplicable, unstoppable phenomenon.

The other pastor, seasoned by experience, pushed gently: "You've built this, and it's okay to say that. You've intentionally and strategically built a very large church."

"We had nothing to do with it," the young pastor insisted.

"Well, not nothing," said the older pastor. "You kept putting up more chairs."

We can get so caught up in pursuing our callings that we sometimes forget there's more than one way to steward that calling. We don't have to pursue bigger and faster. We can take down some chairs . . . Where will you start?

....

....

....

....

....

....

....

....

....

....

We have more authority over our time, energy, and resources than we think. Sometimes we get the balance right and sometimes we don't. In your heart of hearts, what would be the most healthy and whole way for you to express your calling?

....

....

....

....

....

....

....

....

....

....

....

date | |

> You can't have yes without no. Another way to say it: if you're not careful with your yeses, you start to say no to some very important things without even realizing it.

What have you said *yes* to that you can say *no* to instead? For each item, note why this *no* is important to you.

1.
2.
3.
4.
5.
6.
7.
8.
9.
10.

We can learn so much by lookng back at our yeses and our nos: list one struggle, one failure, and one success that you've experienced as you've taken the risk to say no. Why do you think each *no* went the way it did? What does that teach you for the future?

A Struggle

....

....

....

....

....

....

A Failure

....

....

....

....

....

....

A Success

....

....

....

....

....

....

Along the way you will disappoint someone. But here's the good news: you get to decide who you're going to disappoint.

Who are you willing to disappoint? Who are you absolutely not willing to disappoint?

Disappoint	Not Disappoint

Picture your relationships like concentric circles: the inner circle is your spouse, your children, your very best friends. The next circle out is extended family and good friends. The outer edge is people you know but not well.

Aim to disappoint the people at the center as rarely as possible. And then learn to be more comfortable with disappointing the people at the edges—people who do not and should not require your unflagging dedication.

Who are the people in each of your circles?

Each season will come with its own unique purposes and priorities that call out for your time. What are you committing to in *this* season?

....
....
....
....
....
....
....
....
....
....
....
....
....
....
....
....
....
....
....
....
....
....
....
....
....
....

In my experience, you have to start with the outsides—with calendars and concentric circles, lists, saying yes, saying no. Over time, you gain a little breathing room and begin to peel away the next layer, to find the real questions, hurts, and heartaches you've been running from.

As you begin to slow your pace, what new layers and questions and heartaches are you discovering under the surface?

The journey to a simpler, more soulful life, at its core, is a move from dependence on external approval to dependence on God's view of us, His unchanging love. How would you describe God's love for you? What do you think He wants for your life?

Why are you willing to sacrifice your own health and happiness so that people who aren't *you* will think you're doing a good job?

SECTION 2

Tunnels

*"Something needs to change. I can't live like this
anymore. We can't. They can't." . . . I still didn't
understand the solution, but more clearly than ever,
I understood the problem: the hustling that had
so deeply compromised my heart was an effort to
outrun the emptiness and deep insecurity inside me.*

Years ago, our family spent a few days on Kauai in Hawaii, and those days held a true magic for our family. One afternoon we went to Tunnels Beach. It's called Tunnels because the reefs look like tunnels running under the water to the shore. Henry and Aaron went exploring first, while Mac and I played on the beach.

Then Henry came back. "Mom, it's amazing!" And so my darling eight-year-old boy took me by the hand and we swam out through the tunnels. It was absolutely extraordinary, deeply blue with bright coral.

Henry held my hand and pointed things out to me, making sure I saw every brightly colored fish and plant.

I knew that this was one of those moments that a mother keeps with her forever, a snapshot of impossible sweetness. I told myself to stay in it and soak up every second.

And at the very same time, I felt a dagger of such aggressive hatred for myself that I couldn't concentrate. I kept trying to snap myself back into the present, into the wonder, into the beauty, but I couldn't. The wave of deep darkness inside me was too powerful, and while I fought to be fully there, I was swept away by a searing-hot knife slice of self-hatred.

Something unlocked. I couldn't live like that anymore.

When we got home, I talked about it with my people. I kept talking, kept asking for help, kept learning new ways to heal old wounds. And so I began the daily, unglamorous work of rebuilding that strong inner core—replacing that sludgy hatred with love. I'm thankful for that day, when the violence of my emotions became profound enough to shake me into new solutions. That's how we grow, it seems; that's how we submit ourselves to the miraculous . . . by swimming through the tunnels.

For many of us, that's why we do every unhealthy thing we do—to avoid that dark sludge of self-loathing. Have you had moments when you've felt those dark feelings?

Describe how you experience those dark feelings in your body, in your
heart, in your spirit.

....
....
....
....
....
....
....
....
....
....
....
....
....
....
....
....
....
....
....
....
....
....
....
....
....

Many of us feel like these feelings are embarrassing or shameful, but we know that talking about the darkness is what brings us back into the light. Who in your life can you trust with the truth of that darkness?

Silly as it may sound, I begin each
morning by picturing a heart—like a red
cartoon heart. And I train my mind on
the reality of God's unconditional love
for me. For all people, for everything that
He's created. When my mind wanders,
I gently pull it back to the heart. . . .

I'm beginning to see that love is the
truth and the darkness is a lie.

Draw your own heart here. Fill it with the examples of God's unconditional love that speak most strongly to you, the ones that will help you shine a light into your own darkness.

Years ago, a wise friend taught me to picture a bottle of oil-and-vinegar salad dressing when I pray. The vinegar rests on top of the olive oil. When you begin to pray, pour out the vinegar first—the acid of whatever has hurt you, is troubling you, is jangling your nerves or spirit.

Then what you find underneath is the oil, glistening and thick. This is the grounding truth of life with God, that we're connected, that we're not alone. You have to pour out the acid before you get to the richness of the oil, and you can't get there unless you're willing to truly be seen, vinegar and all.

What is the vinegar you need to pour out to God today? What is hard or heavy or bringing pain into your life right now?

Once you poured out the vinegar, what was the oil you found underneath? How did God remind you of His goodness, His faithfulness, His love for you?

Connection with God isn't just through prayer and sermons—it's in poetry and music, silence and imagination. Art and creativity open up a wide and holy space for God to demonstrate His nature to us in all sorts of ways. These are some of my favorite books, authors, poems, and songs, the creations that help draw me closer to God.

Original Blessing by Danielle Shroyer
The Book of Delights by Ross Gay
Georgica Pond by Johnny Swim
The Sun Will Rise by The Brilliance
Pilgrim by David Whyte
Devotions by Mary Oliver

What books, shows, music, movies, poems are medicine for you? Make your own list. Come back and add to this anytime you stumble upon something that feels like prayer or medicine or holiness.

What traditions or practices are you drawn to outside your faith experience? How can you learn from those traditions and incorporate parts of those practices into your faith?

What traditions in your own church do you especially love? What do they mean to you?

It seems that Christians ought to be deeply grounded, living a courageous rhythm of rest, prayer, service, and work. That rhythm is biblical, and it's one Jesus Himself modeled. How do your daily, weekly, and monthly schedules align with that rhythm?

Our rich, historic faith tradition is built on feasts and holidays, Sabbath and evening prayers—a rhythmic, beautiful life with God. Many of us have stomped on the accelerator of our own lives and raced past these traditions. But the pattern remains if you're willing to take it up. What could a Sabbath practice look like in your life?

We are—every one of us—God's children, loved unconditionally and wholly. Is that an easy and natural thing for you to believe about yourself? Or do you sometimes feel that you need to earn God's love through good behavior or performance? Where did that way of thinking come from?

Lectio divina is an ancient practice of immersing yourself in Scripture on a very personal and contemplative level. You select a passage of scripture and then read, reflect, respond, and rest.

1. *Read* the selection and let the words wash over you.
2. Then *reflect*, reading the passage again and again, as you listen and feel for God's nudge or guiding presence.
3. When you have finished, *respond* in whatever way makes sense to you. You can journal or think or pray or just let the Scripture settle into your heart.
4. Finally, *rest* in stillness as the work God began is finished for now.

Choose a verse that speaks to your soul, that reminds you that you are God's beloved child, and try it for yourself. Write your *lectio divina* verses here.

When I look at your heavens, the work
of your fingers, the moon and the stars,
which you have set in place, what is man
that you are mindful of him, and the
son of man that you care for him?

Psalm 8:3

As these words began to take root in me,
as I read and reread them, as I prayed and
listened, I felt my tangled spirit begin to
untangle. I felt my breath slow and deepen.
I felt a part of the natural world, governed
by a good God, created with care and
attentiveness. I felt my daughter-ness, my
place in the family of God. And I exhaled.

date | | |

Here's the truth: sometimes when I think of Jesus, I see a face of such love and such connection that I feel uncomfortable being truly seen, or demonstrating my own deep need. And sometimes my prayers feel more like report cards and apologies and promises to do better. What feelings or beliefs sometimes get in the way when you pray?

We begin to know Jesus in a deeper way when we begin to become comfortable with simply being, with silence, with stillness. He says, "Be still, and know that I am God." (Psalm 46:10). Be still and know. Be still. Be. It starts with *be*. Just be, dear one.

Write a prayer here asking for help you might feel you don't "deserve" to ask for.

Dear Jesus,

....
....
....
....
....
....
....
....
....
....
....
....
....
....

Amen.

I've learned that silence is where the grounding, the healing takes place. Is silence difficult for you? How do you feel in your heart and your body when you practice silence?

In silence you can truly allow yourself to be seen, and in being seen, healing and groundedness begin. Where can you find or build more silence into your days?

-‹‹‹‹-

When I practice allowing myself to be
seen and loved by the God who created
me from dust, I start to carry an inner
stillness back into the noise, like a secret.
When I start to feel the questions, the fear,
the chaos, I can return to that quiet, that
stillness, that grounded place within me.

Let's work on building your quiet place within.
Take five minutes to sit in silence. Picture
yourself removing all the noise and chaos
and business you are usually surrounded by,
until you are standing alone. Imagine God
standing beside you, Jesus on your other side,
the Holy Spirit hovering over you. Imagine
the force of all of that love for you, shielding
you, creating a bubble of stillness and love.

-‹‹‹‹-

What does that feel like? Were you able to return to that place throughout the day?

The rhythm you were created for sounds a lot like your own heartbeat, the rhythm of God, pumping in your chest, the most beautiful song you've ever heard.

Whatever thing you think you can't do without—alcohol, shopping, that number on a scale, the lies, the jealousy, the success—when you release that thing, that's when you'll feel the rhythm you were made to feel. What thing are you fighting to release? What might happen if you let it go?

Take time today to sit in silence, to listen for the groove, for the rhythm of God. What does it sound like to you?

I bought myself a necklace with a tiny star on a fine gold chain—a symbol of nature, of the silent night sky. Several times a day, my fingers find the tiny star around my neck, a reminder to myself that this practice of silence is something difficult and valuable. Do you need a physical reminder of this work you are doing? Is there a symbol that feels significant to you? Draw it here.

When I get out of the city—the noise and chaos, the screaming intensity—then I can see the stars. And they're beautiful.

SECTION 3

Legacy

*The legacy I care most about is the one I'm creating
with the people who know me best—my children, my
husband, my best friends. And I have to make a change.*

A friend of mine wrote a wonderful curriculum, helping people sort through their desires and dreams, and he asked for my help filming it. We began in the morning—goals, memories, the plot points of my childhood and adolescent years. We plugged along, sharing stories, laughing between takes. And then the conversation turned to legacy, the end of life, regret. And with the cameras rolling and the room full of talented, kind people, I looked up at my friend and began to cry.

"I don't want to miss the actual fabric of the interior of my life and the beautiful children growing up right this second in my own home because I'm working to please people somewhere out there. I'm afraid

I'm missing it. I'm afraid I'm doing it wrong, and I want to know that I can change."

My friend paused before he spoke, "You can get this right. It's not too late. You can start again, right now."

In someone else's city, in someone else's home, sitting at someone else's kitchen table, I knew with all certainty that what I longed for was my own table, my own home, my city, my people. I knew that my legacy wasn't what I wanted it to be *yet*, but there was still time to change that. There's time for you too.

Do you feel comfortable and confident saying, "This is who I am, this is who I'm not, this is what I want, this is what I'm leaving behind"? Why or why not?

Write down what you know deep inside yourself: the things you love, the things you know to be true about yourself, and the things you dream about for your life.

This is what I love . . .

This is what's true about me . . .

These are my dreams . . .

You get to tell the truth about what you love and who you are and what you dream about. We'll learn this new path together.

One of the greatest delights in life is walking away from what someone said you should care about and walking *toward* what you truly love—in your heart, in your secret soul. What ways of living have you simply acquiesced to because someone said to or because it seemed smart or practical or easy?

How would you like to change that?

You get to make your life. In fact, you have to. And you can *remake* it too. We get to shape our days and our weeks, and if we don't, they'll get shaped by the wide catchall of "normal" and "typical." What are the best words to describe how *you* want to live?

What do you think your legacy would be if you died today?

In what ways is that the legacy you want to leave?

Who do you want to leave a legacy for?

What do you want your legacy to be?

Who receives the best of your energy and love? How often does your best go to your colleagues at work, to your clients, to acquaintances, or worse yet, to strangers?

How often are you giving your best to the people who love you best,
the people who know you best?

When things are difficult at home, what a lovely thing it is to be loved at work, right? What a lovely and dangerous thing. What an easy escape, into people who think you're great and work that makes you feel valuable. I can master my laptop in a way that I cannot master parenting. I can control my deadlines in a way that I cannot control our marriage. What is your lovely and dangerous escape? What does it give you that you can't easily find at home?

One of the great hazards is quick love, which is actually charm. We get used to smiling, hugging, bantering, practicing good eye contact. And it's easier than true, slow, awkward, painful connection with someone who sees all the worst parts of you. Your act is easy. Being with you, deeply with you, is difficult.

It is better to be loved than admired. It is better to be truly known and seen and taken care of by a small tribe than adored by strangers who think they know you in a meaningful way. We know that's true. But many of us, functionally, have gotten that math wrong in one season or another.

What can you change so that you aren't too exhausted from work, hobbies, or commitments to get down on the floor and play with your toddler or stay in the second hour of a difficult conversation with your spouse?

We often skate past negative feelings, staying busy, putting a positive spin on them. We even ignore our body's signals. I want to encourage you to sit with whatever difficult emotions you are experiencing. Instead of running and distracting and misdiagnosing, sit in silence and let yourself feel the full weight. What root emotion are you experiencing under the anger or tears or panic?

It's very hard to be loved and connected to the people in your home when you're always bringing them your most exhausted self.

What subtle messages is your body sending you, waiting for you to listen?

I frequently pay more attention to how I *should* feel about something than how I actually *do* feel about it. *Should* is a warning sign. We can't build the lives we truly want if we are feeling what we should instead of how we truly feel.

What feelings have you been outrunning lately? Circle any and all that apply.

Fear	Loneliness	Guilt	Worried
Grief	Exhaustion	Helplessness	Nervous
Envy	Resentment	Dread	Craving
Anxiety	Dejection	Shame	Horror
Regret	Despair	Indignation	Relief
Disgust	Anger	Disdain	
Rage	Hatred	Boredom	
Sadness	Self-Loathing	Confusion	

Which of these feelings do you feel most often in this season?

Should is a warning sign.

We may think we're dealing with our negative emotions—outsmarting them, outrunning them—but those emotions tend to be the ones that pop out when we least expect it, wreaking havoc on our days and relationships. Spend a few moments here paying attention to any emotions you may have buried for too long so that they don't manage you and your actions.

We roasted marshmallows in the driveway, watched the stars come out, shot baskets till it was too dark to see a thing. It feels right, more and more often, to let the boys' desires define our decisions—not in every way, but in some. The hours we've spent in the driveway this spring are some of the sweetest we've spent together. Aaron and I aren't homebodies at all, not routine people even a little. We love to travel, love the changes of scenery and adventure. But our boys are teaching us about home, about patterns, about the most meaningful ways to spend our time.

Our home has become more an anchor and less a place to land for a hot minute. How can you help your home feel more like an anchor for your family?

Sometimes brave looks more like staying when you want to leave, telling the truth when you want to change the subject. Sometimes it means climbing a mountain. Sometimes it means staying home. What does brave look like for you in this season?

Brave doesn't always involve grand gestures.

What's the quietest brave thing you've ever done?

What are you bravely building that others might see as boring?

For me, being brave is trusting
that what my God is asking
of me, what my family and
community are asking from
me, is totally different than
what our culture says I
should do. Sometimes brave
looks boring and that's
totally, absolutely okay.

Let's talk for a minute about *perfect*. Perfect is brittle and unyielding, plastic, distant, more image than flesh. It keeps us isolated and exhausted, trying to reach some ideal that never comes. What images of perfection have you been hustling for?

What is the worst that would happen if you let that perfect go? What's the best that could happen?

And so, instead: present. If perfect is plastic, present is rich, loamy soil. It's real and tactile and something you can hold with both hands, something rich and warm. It's the Bible with the battered cover, the journal filled with scribbled, secret dreams. It isn't pretty, necessarily—it isn't supposed to be. Present means we understand that the here and now is sacred, sacramental, threaded through with divinity even in its plainness. Especially in its plainness.

How can you choose to be present over perfect in this season, in your home, with your people?

Present over perfect living is real over image,
connecting over comparing, meaning over mania,
depth over artifice. *Present over perfect* living
is the risky and revolutionary belief that the
world God has created is beautiful and valuable
on its own terms and that it doesn't need to be
zhuzhed up and fancy in order to be wonderful.

Sink deeply into the world as it stands. Breathe
in the smell of rain and the scuff of leaves as
they scrape across driveways on windy nights.
This is where life is, not in some imaginary,
photoshopped dreamland. Here. Now. You,
just as you are. Me, just as I am. This world,
just as it is. This is the good stuff. This is the
best stuff there is. Perfect has nothing on truly,
completely, wide-eyed, open-souled present.

Do you have a physical reminder to help you feel more grounded? What posture or practice could help you feel more connected and present?

SECTION 4

Walking on Water

Here's the thing about filters—they color everything.
Nothing is neutral; nothing escapes them.

A t a recent contemplative gathering, a Jesuit priest led us
through an Ignatian prayer of imagination for the story of
Peter walking on water. Essentially, he read the scripture
aloud, and we imagined ourselves in the story: What did it
smell like? What did it sound like? What character in the story are you?

I felt like I knew this story in such a visceral, familiar way because
of all the times I'd been just like Peter—step out, sink, receive the
scolding. Step out—longer this time! But then inevitably sink, receive
the scolding. The scolding's the worst part.

The gentle priest read the story again, and again, and again. We
listened, exhaled, practiced the prayer of imagination. Again and again.

And there in my chair, I realized that I'd had the story all wrong. I had twisted it through my filter of shame and not being good enough. But then, something clicked and released.

Before Jesus scolds Peter, first He *rescues* him. I always picture the falter, the failure, the scolding, then, finally, the begrudging hand of help.

But the rescue came first! When Peter faltered, Jesus reached out a hand before saying a word. For a girl who's been failing and faltering all her life, bracing for the scolding, enduring the disappointment until the hand is finally extended and I am safe, this changes everything.

And the scolding? It's not a scolding at all. It's a loving post-game analysis—*Hey, pal, what happened out there? How can we, together, help you*

> The shame glasses I wear almost all the time mean that every story looks like shame to me. Every punchline, every plot twist— they're all the same: you're *not good enough.*

stand? It's so loving, so parental, so protective . . . why haven't I ever seen it this way?

Because I'm trained for shame, and I see it everywhere. But what if it's not there? What if all my life I've been trying to walk with an imagined Jesus who reprimands me while I'm drowning and grabs me at the last second, rolling His eyes, instead of the real Jesus, the One who rescues first?

How many other stories from Scripture have I twisted? How many images of God have I constructed out of my own wounds? And what would happen if I went back and found the narrative fundamentally altered?

The shame glasses I wear mean that every story looks like shame to me. What filters do you see the world through?

Is there a particular Bible story you've struggled with over the years?
What is it, and why does it trigger your filters?

Return to that Bible story and try the Ignatian prayer of imagination for yourself. (Picture yourself there: What did it smell like? What did it sound like? What character in the story are you?) Does it reveal anything new?

What are some of the images of God and Jesus you may have constructed out of your own wounds? Are those images accurate?

I find my heart is drawn so entirely
to only two places: the table and
the water. Our home and the edge
of the big water, the two most
sacred places I've ever known.

One way to look at it: Communion
and baptism. I'm a table person, a
bread and wine person. And I'm a
water person, profoundly. All my life,
I've felt most deeply myself around
the table and on the shore, the bread
and the wine and the water.

Which places are you drawn to? Which places or seasons are the most sacred for you?

I've burned down my long-held expectations of who I had to be, because I could no longer stand the distance those expectations created between God and me, the people I love and me, the beauty of the world and me.

What do you need to burn down in your life to make space for a new way of living?

What commitments, expectations, roles, and structures in your life could be shifted in order to bring about healthy changes?

When you leave behind busyness,
exhaustion, codependence,
compulsive anything, you can
see the cracks and brokenness in
your relationships for what they
really are—and you realize that
you have to either fix the cracks
or let the connection break.

Look around. Which cracks do you need to repair? Which connections do you need to let go of, to let break?

Have you ever recognized in yourself a deep jealousy toward a friend? Perhaps her schedule, or her family, or her day that feels lighter than yours, easier. *Must be nice*, you think. If we tiptoe past the disdain, past the envy, we often find longing—for a life that feels light, right-sized for our strengths and limitations.

What or who makes you think, *Must be nice*? Why?

What realization or longing might your jealousy lead you to if you're brave enough to listen to it before pushing it away?

There's something so human about
feeling embarrassed, about wanting
to hide, about wanting to conceal and
control the out-of-control and painful
things about our lives and stories and
families. Love, though, doesn't allow
hiding. Love invites whole selves
and whole stories out into the light.
Friendship sees into us, into our secrets,
into our elaborate games and excuses.
Friendship carries all this mess together
so that you don't have to hide, so that
you carry it together. What a miracle!

What are your friends helping you carry in this season?

Think about each of your people. What are you helping them carry?

Name (...............)

Name (...............)

Name (...............)

Name (...............)

Name (...............)

We're all so much more similar than we are different. Our secrets are largely the same. Our fears are largely the same. Marriages crack, addictions take hold, families break, irreversible decisions are made. No one is exempt. Are there secrets you have been trying to carry on your own?

Who can you trust to carry these things with you?

You don't have to sacrifice your spirit, your joy, your soul, your family, your marriage on the altar of any sort of work. Just because you have the capacity to do something doesn't mean you have to do it. Often, when we look back at our regrets, we remember those moments when we allowed someone else to dictate our path, instead of listening to our own values and desires.

When you look back at the last few years, what are some things that you regret? Why? Is there a pattern you can recognize?

We are responsible for stewarding our own lives, our desires and limitations, our capacities and longings. How would you describe the capacity you have believed you needed to have?

....
....
....
....
....
....
....
....
....
....

Revel in the smallness of your own capacity. *This is who I am. This is all I have to give you.* And then tend that small stream that is yours to nurture so you can offer first to the people you love most.

....
....
....
....
....
....
....
....
....
....

How would you describe the capacity you *actually* have?

Do you know what it's like to be rested? Truly rested? What does it feel like in your body? In your heart?

Do you know what it's like to feel connected, in deep and lovely ways, to the people you love most? What does that feel like, in your body and in your heart?

Have you experienced the sweetness of working hard and then stopping, realizing that your body and your spirit have carried you far enough and now they need to be tended to? What does that feel like?

We're not building castles or monuments; we're building souls and families. So let's spend our lives on meaning, on connection, on love, on freedom. What does this look like for you?

At the end of it all, at the center of it all, that's the whole of who I am: this God-ward heart. Amen.

It takes time and practice to shift down to a slower speed—to less—and to stay there. Try it with various things in your life today. List the challenge and circle whether you had trouble or made progress. Why do you think each attempt went the way it did? What does that teach you for the future?

The Challenge:

HAD TROUBLE   MADE PROGRESS

The Challenge:

HAD TROUBLE   MADE PROGRESS

The Challenge:

HAD TROUBLE   MADE PROGRESS

date | |

The Challenge: ....

                            HAD TROUBLE   MADE PROGRESS

The Challenge: ....

                            HAD TROUBLE   MADE PROGRESS

The Challenge: ....

                            HAD TROUBLE   MADE PROGRESS

SECTION 5

Living in Time

After a lifetime of believing that the voices that mattered were Out There, *approving or disapproving of me, I'm learning to trust the voice within, the voice of God's Spirit, the whisper of my own soul.*

am deeply committed to living in the present, to pouring out my time lavishly for this moment, to choosing how I spend each *right now* with care and intention. I used to spend so much time living in some uncertain "perfect" future that will never exist, hustling and proving and pushing to try to get there. I never want to do that again. But to get back to existing in my life as it is *right now*, I had to be willing to go back first to find the truest version of me, the girl I'd callously left behind in my hurry to get ahead.

There's tremendous value in traveling back to our essential selves, the loves and skills and passions God planted inside us long ago. When I look at my life these days, I see the threads of passion and identity

I've carried through my whole life: books and reading, people and connection, food and the table. These are the things I've always loved, and they continue to bring me great joy and fulfillment.

Think about your adolescent self, your child self, the "you" you've always been. God imprinted a sacred, beautiful collection of passions and capacities right onto your heart: What do you love? What does your passion bubble over for?

So much of adulthood is peeling off the layers of expectation and pressure, and protecting those precious things that lie beneath. We live in a culture that shouts, that prescribes rather narrowly what it means to be a woman, what it means to be a success, what it means to live a valuable life. But that's not life. That's not where the fullness of joy and meaning are found.

Those things are found only in living out your life fully present, moment by moment, just as you were created to be, weird and wonderful, imperfect and messy and lovely.

Of all the things we learn to leave behind, one of the heaviest is the opinions of others. Whose opinions are you still clutching with white knuckles? Why are they so difficult to release?

Pleasing is such a fraught
and freighted word, it seems,
saccharine and over-sweet.
Let's do so much more than
simply please people. Let's
see them and love them
and delight them, look
deeply into their eyes.

People, individual people, matter more to me than ever. I'm giving more focused time to the people I love than I ever have: eye to eye, uninterrupted, deeply connected. Who are the people who matter most to you?

Are there people in your life who trigger your need to please? How can you navigate this together to get to a healthier place or, if that's not possible, how can you add some healthy distance in that relationship?

....

....

....

....

....

....

....

....

....

....

Make a plan to prioritize your people and spend less time and energy on the opinions of people who don't matter to you.

....

....

....

....

....

....

....

....

....

....

What would your life be like if your days were studded by tiny, completely unproductive, silly, nonstrategic, wild and beautiful five-minute breaks, reminders that your days are for loving and learning and laughing, not for pushing and planning, reminders that it's all about the heart, not about the hustle?

We default to hustle mode all too often. Hustle is the opposite of heart. One of the things we can learn to do is to play—to purposely waste time, to strategically avoid strategy, for five minutes at a time. Have no purpose—*on purpose*. What are some of the ways you like to play?

Many of us stay up far later than we should—wringing the last moments out of the day, pouring the last glass of wine, reading one more chapter, tending to that last task before bed, having just one more conversation.

Do you need more sleep? In what ways do you struggle to shut down at night?

....
....
....
....
....
....
....
....
....
....
....
....
....
....
....
....
....
....
....
....
....
....
....
....
....

Proper pajamas can be a breakthrough—when it's time for bed, tell your body it's time to rest by putting on your pajamas, clothes specifically made for home, for quiet, for sleep. Do you own real pajamas? How do they differ from your regular clothes or workout clothes? What other nighttime routines signal your body and mind that it's time for rest?

When I begin the day in quiet on the porch, it connects me to God through prayer, and it connects me to God through His creation. There's something wonderful and healthy and healing about being outside, something my own life is crying out for. Being outside reminds me of life and God and growth, and the energy and motion of nature, all things I forget so easily when I spend my life too much indoors, too much in a world of laptops and laundry and lists.

How can you intentionally incorporate rituals like starting the day in creation to help you set new rhythms of care?

Sacred margin at the beginning and end of the day—letting the transitions between sleeping and waking be a little gentler—can be transformative.

Are you a night owl or an early bird? Stay up too late and hit snooze too often? Or go to bed and wake up with the sun?

Do you want to continue in that pattern? Why or why not?

I love how the Catholic and Jewish traditions connect to real, touchable, material life. What we own, what we touch, what we carry: these things matter. What we surround ourselves with, how we regard our material possessions and our physical selves: these things matter.

How do you feel about your possessions? Do you have too little, exactly what you need, way more than you need, or so much that you are drowning in it? Explain why.

Simplifying your closet can leave you feeling lighter and more like yourself. Do you have a closet full of clothes you don't wear? It's time to figure out why. What colors do you like to wear? Which silhouettes and styles do you feel most comfortable in? Which accessories help you feel happy? Now it's time to get rid of most everything that doesn't fit those parameters.

I like living in our home when it's less full of stuff. It's easier to get dressed and enjoy time in the kitchen when I have fewer choices. The simplicity feels spacious and inspiring, like I can draw a clean breath. Where and how can *less* serve you in this season?

Room (............) ....

....

Room (............) ....

....

Room (............) ....

....

Room (............) ....

....

Room (............) ....

....

Room (............) ....

....

Room (............) ....

....

Room (............) ....

....

Room (............) ....

....

Room (............) ....

....

Room (............) ....

....

Let's make a plan for less. Start with something that feels easy to you.
What will it be?

How will you get to less?

Where will the excess go?

I've done the same simplifying in my kitchen, and now it's filled only with things we use and love. What room in your home would benefit from this exercise? Use this chart to help you purge, pare down, simplify.

Love	Use Often	Donate

I make better decisions when
I make fewer decisions. The
ambient noise of my life gets
quieter when there's less stuff
in my life and fewer decisions
to make about that stuff.
And in the newfound silences
is space for connection,
rest, listening, learning.

How much time are you spending each day, each week managing stuff? Which stuff? What could you spend that time doing if you had less to manage?

I'm committed to practicing hospitality—the offering of grace and nourishment—not just to other people, but also to myself. How do you feel about your body? Are you offering it grace and nourishment? How and why?

Let's live lightly, freely, courageously, surrounded only by what brings joy, simplicity, and beauty.

I'm going to both take up
space and create space—
for my body and also
for my sadness and my
longing and my anger.

Sometimes we feel beautiful, radiant and lovely, and other times we feel stuck and icky and less than—that's how it is to have a body. Write down some of those feelings here, the good and the bad.

What does it look like to practice hospitality to your own body? You can rest; you can be nourished; you can be loved. We can show hospitality even to the fact that sometimes we have complicated feelings about our bodies. How can you practice hospitality to your feelings about your body?

God's voice thunders in marvelous ways; he does great things beyond our understanding. He says to the snow, "Blanket the earth," and to the rain shower, "Soak the whole countryside!"

Job 37:5–6 MSG

God says to the snow, "Blanket the earth." That's it. Just do one thing. Just fall. And then he says to the rain shower, "Soak the whole countryside!" Essentially, He's saying: just do the thing I've actually created you to do. You're rain, so rain. You're snow, so snow.

God is asking you to be the thing He's already created you to be. Do the thing you love, the thing you've been created to do. What are those things you do effortlessly and with the ease and lightness of falling snow?

So many of us twist ourselves up in knots trying desperately to be something else, someone else, some endless list of qualities and capabilities that we think will make us loved or safe or happy. What do you need to leave behind in order to recover that essential self that God created?

You are also loved and seen by our holy God. How will you let that truth help propel you forward into the life you've been dreaming of?

Throwing Candy

*I had an experience a couple summers ago that
changed everything for me. . . . Every once in a while
we have these experiences that slice our lives into
before and after, and this was one of those for me.*

A friend of a friend invited me to a retreat. There was lots of space and silence. The stars were so bright, and the layers of stress and regret and toughness slipped off one by one, until there I was, just me. And without that shell, I could feel everything with such clarity. For the first time in forever, I was really paying attention.

One of the traditions of this place is that when you see kayakers in the water, you stop and throw candy to them. Because it's fun. If you knew me in my twenties, you'd say, that kind of thing is *so Shauna*. She's totally the candy-throwing type.

One afternoon, the kayakers crossed in front of our dock while about a million other things were happening. Two powerboats and a sailboat were all docking at once, and a few paddle boarders and swimmers were trying not to get in the way. All at the same time.

But our host—the one who owned all the stuff that was about to crash—stopped and sprinted down the dock to get the lollipops. I panicked because it seemed so irresponsible. He threw candy, right in the middle of it. And everything was fine.

I began to sob.

Because I used to throw candy, right in the middle of it all. I used to throw candy no matter what. I used to be warm and whimsical and silly.

And then I became the kind of person who threw candy as long as it didn't get in the way of being responsible, after all the work was done and lunches were made.

And then it was *never* the right time to throw candy.

Then, the worst thing: I became the kind of person who made fun of candy-throwers . . . *Please—who has time?*

What a loss—for me, for my family, for our community, for all the joy and laughter we missed out on because I was busy being busy.

Are you the kind of person who throws candy? Why or why not?

What is appealing about being the candy-throwing type to you? What about it might scare you or feel uncomfortable?

I don't want to get to the end of my
life and look back and realize that
the best thing about me was I was
organized. That I executed well,
that I ran a tight ship, that I never
missed a detail. I want to look back
and remember all the times I threw
candy, even when it didn't make sense.
Especially when it didn't make sense.

Where in your life could you start throwing candy? How?

Every new season of life is an invitation to leave behind the things of the season before, the trappings and traps that have long expired. What are those things for you?

How can you answer the invitation in front of you?

Look at your deepest dreams and who you've always been—the things you love even though no one else does, the times in your life when you feel the most beautiful, even if no one else thinks so. How can you make room in your life for those things? For moments like those?

Things I Love:

....

....

....

....

....

....

....

Times I Feel the Most Beautiful:

....

....

....

....

....

....

....

....

Plan to Experience Those Moments More Often:

....

....

....

....

....

....

....

....

What is your greatest dream for your life?

What would it look like to follow that dream?

What might stand in the way of following that dream?

....
....
....
....
....
....
....
....
....
....
....
....

How do you picture God's unbreakable, unshakeable, unconditional love for you? Write or draw it here.

When we begin our days drenched in love—that centering awareness of our worth and connection to God—our days are different. We don't have to scramble or hustle. Fear dissipates. We're left with warmth, creativity, generosity. We can rest. We can fail. We can admit need and weakness. We can exhale.

One part of this journey is learning to say no. But we don't want it to be the knee-jerk response to all of life. The response to pressure and expectations: no. But the response to beauty and freedom and soulfulness and life lived in God's wild and expansive love? Yes, yes, yes. Always yes. What does yes mean to you?

My favorite sweatshirt says SAY YES . . .
a reminder of this sweet, wide-open way
of living, wholehearted, connected, wholly
there. So does a piece of art on my wall,
a post-in on my desk, and a tattoo on my
arm: reminders everywhere I look of YES.

Saying yes means not hiding. It means being seen in all your imperfections and insecurities. Saying yes is doing scary things without a guarantee that they'll go perfectly. Saying yes is telling the truth even when it's weird or sad or impossibly messy. Saying yes is inviting chaos and also possibility. Saying yes is building a new future, regardless of the past. Saying yes is jumping in anyway. What are you ready to say yes to after a season of saying no?

Think about your closest relationships—your spouse, a dear friend, a close family member. Are you comfortable having the hard conversations that grow these relationships? The stuff we're usually afraid to say out loud loses its power once we share it. Here are some topics and questions to get you started:

What's the best part of your relationship?

....
....
....
....
....
....
....
....

What's the trickiest or most difficult part?

....
....
....
....
....
....
....
....
....

What could you do to strengthen the relationship?

What helps bridge distance between you when it grows?

What ways of living and interacting help you connect deeply?

What are you most afraid of in your relationship? About yourself?

What do you both want for your lives, together and separately?

Some of us feel called to the work we get paid for. Others of us feel called to the work we squeeze into the margins. Whatever that is for you, what fuels or motivates that work?

....
....
....
....
....
....
....
....
....
....
....

Why this career? This hobby? This pursuit? This art?

....
....
....
....
....
....
....
....
....
....
....
....
....

As you've gone through this guided journal and begun the process of letting go of perfection, hustling, and achievement, how has it affected your approach to your work?

....

....

....

....

....

....

....

....

....

....

....

What fuels your work when it's no longer about addiction to achievement?

....

....

....

....

....

....

....

....

....

....

What do you wish you could go back and tell yourself ten years ago?

....
....
....
....
....
....
....
....
....
....
....

What would your ten-years-ago self think of the life you've been living?

....
....
....
....
....
....
....
....
....
....
....
....
....

What would she think of what you are remaking your life into?

When you imagine your soul, what do you picture? Describe or draw that image here.

Do you feel connected to your soul? In what ways?

Our souls are what allow us to connect—with God, with other people, with nature, with art. Without a soul, you can walk and drive and sleep, but you can't love, you can't weep, you can't feel. You can't make great art—or at least not for long.

A soul is not required for a robot. Or for a machine. Or for a set of ideas or theories. But a soul is profoundly necessary for a human. It's from our souls that we love, that we feel, that we create, that we connect.

In three of the four Gospels, Jesus asks, "What good is it for someone to gain the whole world, yet forfeit their soul?" (Mark 8:36 NIV). The whole world, in this context, is essentially all the things you've ever wanted— whatever success means to you, or the good life, or what it looks like to live the dream. What is your version of that?

As you've pursued that dream or vision, has it cost you anything?

....
....
....
....
....

> What kills a soul? Exhaustion, secret keeping, image management. And what brings a soul back from the dead? Honesty, connection, grace.

....
....
....
....

How do you feel about love these days? God's love for you? Your love for your people? Your love for yourself?

....
....
....
....
....
....
....
....
....
....
....
....

Who is getting the best of you these days? Why?

The most beautiful, well-
tended, truly nurtured and
nourished parts of my life
are the innermost ones,
not the flashy public ones.
That's just as it should be.

Have you found the things you've longed for?

What new beliefs, routines, and instincts helped you get there?

If we just keep coming back to
the silence, if we keep grounding
ourselves, as often as we need to, in
God's wild love, if we keep showing
up and choosing to be present in
both the mess and in the delight, we
will find our way home, even if the
road is winding and full of fits and
starts. We will find our way home.

Conclusion

his is what I know: the journey away from hustling and competing and toward grace, rest, and connection has changed every part of my life. I walked away from exhaustion as a way of life and toward subtle beauty and silliness and quiet. I faced some regrets, some fears, some deep faults. And I rediscovered some of the brighter, better parts of me and reclaimed a vision of how I want to live the rest of my days and years—more about people and less about performance, more about heart and less about hustle.

I feel prouder of my smaller, simpler, quieter, more connected life than I ever did when all of life was screaming along. The love we're all looking for isn't found in the hustle. We can't prove it or earn it or compete for it. We can only make space for it, listen for it, travel to the depths of our souls, where the very spirit of God has made His home—that's where we'll find it, where you'll find it.

You'll find it in the faces of the people who've known you all your life, who sit around your table every week, the children whose noses you kiss while they're sleeping. You'll find it in prayer, when you sit in silence, sensing the presence of Christ resurrected.

This is what I've found: there is a way of living that is so sweet, so full, so whole and beautiful that you'll never want to go back once you've tasted it. It's better here, here in the place of love.

I am so excited for you to taste that sweetness for yourself, to see your own life steeped in love and connection and simplicity and grace upon grace. I'm cheering you on every step of the way—as you're learning to say no, becoming brave enough to disappoint people, trusting your own voice, and understanding God's unconditional love for each one of us.

Whatever passage you're facing—entering your twenties or your sixties, facing life alone for the first time in a long time or learning the new dance of partnership, becoming a parent or becoming an empty nester, leaving student life behind or becoming a student once again—has the potential to be your sea-change, your invitation to leave behind what's not essential and travel deeply into the heart of things. My prayer for you is this: as you travel, you'll feel how wildly loved you are and then show that love to everyone you encounter. There is so much life and peace and goodness in a slower, grace-soaked way of living. It inspires me to know that so many of us are walking this path together.

I'm learning to silence the noise, around me and within me, and let myself be seen and loved, not for what I produce but for the fact that I have been created by the hands of a holy God, like every other thing on this earth, equally loved, equally seen.

Spend a few minutes reflecting on the journey you've taken as you've made your way through these pages. What have you learned? What have you left behind? What new practices or ideas will you bring into the next season of your life?

Present Over Perfect

Leaving Behind Frantic for a Simpler, More Soulful Way of Living

Shauna Niequist

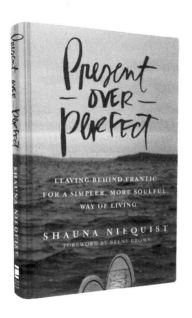

New York Times bestselling author Shauna Niequist invites you to consider the landscape of your own life and what it might look like to leave behind the pressure to be perfect and begin the life-changing practice of simply being present—in the middle of the mess and the ordinariness of life.

As she puts it, "A few years ago, I found myself exhausted and isolated, my soul and body sick. I was tired of being tired, burned out on busy. And it seemed almost everyone I talked with was in the same boat: longing for connection, meaning, depth, but settling for busy. I am a wife, mother, daughter, sister, friend, neighbor, writer, and I know all too well that settling feeling. But over the course of the last few years, I've learned a way to live, marked by grace, love, rest, and play. And it's changing everything. *Present Over Perfect* is an invitation to this journey that changed my life. I'll walk this path with you, a path away from frantic pushing and proving, and toward your essential self, the one you were created to be before you began proving and earning for your worth."

Shauna offers an honest account of what led her to begin this journey and a compelling vision for an entirely new way to live: soaked in grace, rest, silence, simplicity, prayer, and connection with the people who matter most to us.

Available in stores and online!